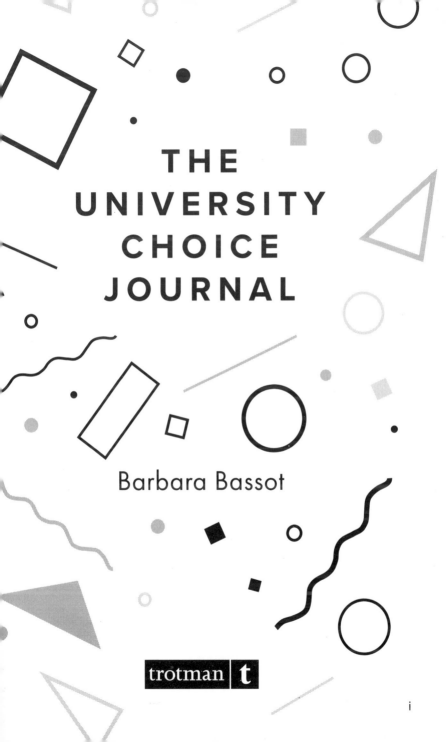

THE
UNIVERSITY
CHOICE
JOURNAL

Barbara Bassot

trotman | t

The University Choice Journal
This first edition published in 2017 by Trotman Education,
an imprint of Crimson Publishing Ltd, 21d Charles Street, Bath,
BA1 1HX.

© Crimson Publishing Ltd, 2017

Author: Barbara Bassot

British Library Cataloguing in Publication Data
A catalogue record for this book is available from the British
Library

ISBN: 978 1 911067 64 1

Designed and typeset by Burville-Riley
Printed and bound by Thomson Press India Ltd.

CONTENTS

ACKNOWLEDGEMENTS

I would like to express my sincere thanks to everyone who helped me in the process of bringing *The University Choice Journal* into fruition; first, my colleagues Chris Targett and Malcolm Scott at CXK, and Louise Badelow and Jenny Douse for their help in the research process. In particular, I would like to thank the students of Astor College, Dover, St George's Church of England Foundation School, Broadstairs, Newstead Wood School, Orpington and Gravesend Grammar School for sharing their ideas for the content of this book and for giving me permission to use their quotes. I would also like to thank Marc Bassot for his careful proofreading. Finally, I would like to thank my Commissioning Editor, Della Oliver, for her belief in the project and for giving me the opportunity to fulfil one of my long-term ambitions in writing this book.

INTRODUCTION

Welcome to *The University Choice Journal.* If you are reading this book, it's because you have decided you want to go to university. Applying to university is a challenging process which can be daunting too. You may be in the sixth form at school or college, or in further education, and feel that you need help to think through the steps you need to take; if so, you've come to the right place!

Of course, there are other options that you could consider after completing your current studies. You could look for work, start an apprenticeship, take a vocational course or do some voluntary work near home or overseas to build your CV. Each of these can be a good option, depending on what you want to achieve in the future. But for the purposes of this book, the assumption is that you have already decided that you want to apply to university.

What makes university choice challenging?

Many students say that the process of university choice is challenging and here are some of the reasons why.

1. It's complex – thinking about which university you want to go to involves lots of different things, such as what to study, where to study.

2. It's time consuming – it takes up a lot of time, and usually needs to be done when you have a lot of academic work to do as well.

3. It's stressful – the process has key deadlines that must be met to ensure your success. Deadlines have the horrible habit of creeping up on us when we put things off!

4. It's a big thing – at the last count there were approximately 37,000 different courses on offer at universities in the UK alone! The amount of information available can soon make you feel that you have 'information overload'.

5. It may be the first big decision you have made about your future – most of us make decisions by looking back at our previous experiences and evaluating them. With our first big decision that just isn't possible.

6. It can be scary – many students worry about making a mistake and choosing the wrong thing.

7. It forces you to think about change – most of us are 'creatures of habit' and prefer things to stay as they are. If you're happy at the moment, you may be excited about the future or you may not want things to change. Even if you dislike what you are doing now, this is often better than reaching out into the unknown.

8. It's a key part of your career development – this means it's abstract and can be difficult to imagine.

But remember, with the right help and support you will be able to make positive choices that will help you to take some steps forward towards your future.

University choice is about career development

Things to do with careers can be difficult to understand because they are abstract. As you think about leaving school or college, you are beginning a process of transition and taking your next steps on a journey towards your future. This can at times be stressful and so, understanding more about it will help you to cope well as you progress. While it is a challenging process, it is also an exciting one, where you can take some big strides forward in your learning and development.

There are three key elements to effective career learning and development (Bassot et al., 2014).

1. Career happiness – this means focusing on what you want and what will make you happy.

2. Career resilience – this means being able to 'bounce back' from any disappointments and being positive about the challenges that university choice presents.

3. Career growth – in order to develop you need to focus on your next steps, so you can move forward effectively.

For many people, going to university will be their next step, giving them the chance to do something they enjoy, and is also likely to give them opportunities to build resilience.

The purpose of this book

The University Choice Journal is a tool to help you to think things through; it will help you to understand more about yourself and what you want to do next. Why is this important? Going to university is the next vital step in your development, and is likely to have an important impact on what you do in the future. Everyone knows that going to university is expensive; if you had a lot of money to spend on a round-the-world trip or an expensive car, you would think things through carefully. Going to university is no different from this. This book will help you to consider many of the factors that influence how you make your choices. This will put you into a stronger position to make good decisions.

How to use this book

This book can be used in a number of ways to help you in the university choice process. You can work through it from start to finish, or select the topics that are the most relevant and interesting at a particular time. The following points are here to guide you.

It's a book that you write in

The most important thing to understand is that this is a book designed for you to write in. But why? Writing by hand is a cognitive process; it helps us to process our thoughts, which develops our ideas and understanding. Neuroscience shows that writing stimulates a particular part of the human brain – the reticular activating system (RAS) – and this makes us concentrate and focus our attention on what we are writing about. Our ideas develop as we write about them. In addition, we are much more likely to remember something when we have written it down, especially when we have a lot going on. We can also go back to it later; it's easy to assume that we will remember things, but we often don't, especially when we have lots of new things to explore.

It's portable

You can put it in your bag or backpack and remember to use it whenever you want or need to. This might be while you are travelling to school or college, doing your research or on university visits.

It's a place to store important things

Once you get going with your research, you will soon start to gather important information that you will want to refer to later. You can keep some of this in this book; in addition, you may well want to keep a paper file, or files on your laptop or smartphone. There are also exercises and activities that will help you to sift through the information you are gathering. Here your hand-written notes will save you lots of valuable time in the future.

How this book is organised

The University Choice Journal is organised in three parts.

Part I is broken down into 10 themes. Each theme starts with a brief introduction and is followed by some relevant topics. There are activities to complete and spaces to write in. At the end of each theme section you will find a page for further notes.

Part II contains further exercises, along with more blank pages for reflective writing. These contain prompts to help you to think through important areas in more depth.

Part III contains some useful materials to help you to store important information that you may well need to have at your fingertips when you are making decisions in the near future.

Many people find that the time they spend writing reflectively is time well invested. I hope that you will find *The University Choice Journal* helpful. By using this book, you are taking the next step in your development – congratulations!

Barbara Bassot

Brace yourself!

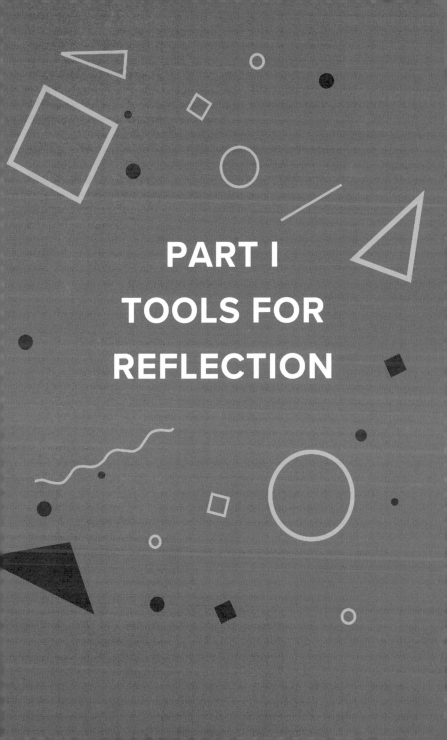

PART I
TOOLS FOR
REFLECTION

Why university?

This section will help you to:

- think about why you want to go to university
- begin to reflect on what is important to you and what will make you happy
- examine your strengths, weaknesses and interests
- explore who might be influencing your choices
- set some goals to help you to move forward.

THEME 1.1

Why do I want to go to university?

Before you start the application process, it is good to be clear
about why you want to go to university. It's important that your
reasons are clear, as this will help when it comes to making some
key decisions. People want to go to university for a range of
reasons, and here are some of the common ones.

- It will help me get the job I want.
- It will help me to become better qualified.
- It will help me to keep my options open.
- I'm not sure what I want to do in the future, so it seems like a good idea for now.
- The social life will be good.
- I want to move away from home.
- I'll make lots of new friends.
- All my friends are going.
- My brother/sister went.
- My parents/carers want me to.
- My teachers want me to.
- I can't think of anything else to do right now, so I may as well.

Clearly some of these reasons are good and valid, while others may
not be.

 # *Try this*

Looking at the list on the opposite page, which do you think
are positive reasons for going to university and which could be
negative? Don't forget that what is a positive reason for one person
might be a negative reason for someone else (e.g. living away from
home). Remember too that this is about what is important for you,
not anybody else.

Now make a list of the reasons why you want to go to university
and rank them in the order of their importance.

What about my values?

Whatever decisions we make in life, it is important to understand what makes us happy; the same applies to the process of university choice. Understanding what makes us happy (and equally, what makes us unhappy) means being aware of our values. Taken literally, our values are the things we value; the things that are important to us. If we find ourselves in a situation where these are compromised, we are likely to feel unhappy.

Values vary from person to person and here is a list of some common ones.

- Achievement
- Ambition
- Belonging
- Care for the environment
- Challenge
- Community
- Creativity
- Curiosity
- Determination
- Enjoyment
- Enthusiasm

- Family orientation
- Helping society
- Honesty
- Independence
- Loyalty
- Making a difference
- Reliability
- Self-reliance
- Tolerance
- Usefulness

It is good to spend a bit of time thinking about the things that are really important to you as they can act as a guide when you are making your decisions.

✏️ *Try this*

From the list on the opposite page, think about the things that are important to you as you begin the university choice process. What do you feel is missing from the list that you would like to add?

THEME 1.3

My strengths, weaknesses and interests

Understanding your strengths, weaknesses and interests will help you as you think about university choice. It is good to consider the following questions.

- What am I really good at? This could include the subjects where you gain your highest marks, areas of sport, music, art and so on, where you excel, or anything where people might say 'you are great at that'.

- What am I not so good at? This could include subjects you dropped or had to re-sit, or things you decided to give up because you found them too difficult.

- What do I love to do? This could include things in school or college, or outside.

All of these give us insights into what kind of person we are and what might suit us well in the future. In relation to university choice it's also important to consider the very broad question of whether you see yourself as an academic person or a more practical one. This could have a big impact on the kind of course you might choose (see Theme 3).

> Take it slowly, don't try to rush the process; take your time, look around and then decide what you want to do.

✏ *Try this*

Speak to some people who know you well (e.g. friends, family, teachers) and ask them for some feedback on how they see you. Do they see you as an academic person or someone who is more practical? Or possibly both? Write some notes here.

THEME 1.4

Who is influencing my decisions?

Whether we want to admit it or not, many of us are influenced by the people close to us when it comes to making decisions. This is not necessarily always a bad thing, but when the decision we make is in effect no longer ours, this should ring some alarm bells for us. Here are some examples to think about.

- *My older brother or sister went to university and did X. They enjoyed it and now have a really good job, so that's what I want to do.* Of course this might be the case for them and it might be for you too, but equally it might not.

- *My parents/carers are expecting me to go and do X and I feel I might let them down if I choose to do something different.* Are you sure this is the case, or might you be making an assumption?

- *My boyfriend/girlfriend is going to X, so that's where I want to go too.* You will both meet lots of new people and being close enough to visit can be a good option.

- *My favourite teacher went to X, loved it and thinks it would suit me too.* They probably went there at least a few years ago and things may well have changed.

While it is important to consider what other people think (and remember, they will hopefully be supporting you in various ways), overall the most important thing is that this is what **you** want to do. After all, once your decisions are made, you're the one that will have to do it, not them! Being sure that it's what you want means you will be much more likely to work hard and succeed.

 *Try this*

Make a list of the people who are influencing your decisions. Now think about whether the influence they are having is too little or too great.

Planning my time

Planning our time helps us to achieve more and to have a sense of purpose. In relation to university choice, there are some key deadlines that need to be met. At the beginning of the process you may well feel that you have plenty of time, but time can go very quickly, so it's important not to be caught out. In addition, a number of courses fill up some time before the final application deadline, so applying ahead of that is a very good thing to do.

One way to plan is to 'begin with the end in mind' (Covey, 2004) and work back from there. So, looking forward, where do you hope to be in a year or two's time? Now think about the important landmarks on the way, e.g. when you get your course results; the final deadline for applications; the deadline for applications that you have set so as to give yourself a good chance of receiving an offer of a place; the deadline you have set for writing your personal statement for your UCAS application; dates for university visits and so on.

Planning ahead is vital for your success – remember the phrase 'to fail to plan is to plan to fail'.

✏ *Try this*

Draw a timeline for the coming months detailing the things
you want to do and by when. Share this with someone (e.g.
your personal tutor) to make sure you haven't missed anything
important. You will want to add to this as time goes on.

 *Further notes*

THEME 2

What makes a good decision?

This section will help you to:

- think about different decision-making styles
- consider how to make logical decisions
- think about how you might use emotions when making decisions
- consider how you may sometimes limit what you could be capable of
- focus on the next steps.

Decision-making styles

People make decisions in all sorts of different ways, and there is not a single or correct way of making a good decision. Here are nine examples of different styles, listed in no particular order.

1. Impulsive – spontaneous, takes the first option that comes up.
2. Fatalistic – believes that fate will decide and 'what will be, will be'.
3. Compliant – heavily influenced by other people and tends to 'fall in line' with their views and wishes.
4. Delayed – always puts off making decisions.
5. Agonising – thinks everything through in minute detail.
6. Planning – logical, rational and balanced.
7. Intuitive – focuses on feelings and 'gut instincts'.
8. Escapist – avoids making decisions whenever possible.
9. Play it safe – takes the easiest route.

Each of these decision-making styles has strengths and weaknesses, but some may well have more strengths than others. For example, the Escapist style might sound fine for a while, but failing to make decisions will probably catch up with us sooner or later. Many people make their university choices by using a combination of the styles, but as you will see, taking a strategic approach is very important too (see Theme 5).

✎ *Try this*

Think of an important decision you have made in the past. How did you make it? Which of the styles did you use and why?

A good decision is a logical one

Many people argue that a good decision is a logical or rational one. Certainly if you take time to think through various aspects of a decision, you are less likely to make mistakes and end up doing something that you regret further down the line. So, how do you make a logical decision in relation to university choice? Here are some pointers.

- Do your research – there is such a lot of information out there that you will need to start this early.
- Think about the pros and cons – all options have advantages and disadvantages and being aware of what you think will be important.
- Discuss things with relevant people – this will help your thoughts to become clearer.

All of these things will help you make a more logical decision and, of course, using this journal should help too. But remember, this is only one way of making a decision, and, as we will see, other aspects are important too.

✎ *Try this*

Write a list of the pros and cons of going to university. Remember, this is about what you think, not anyone else.

It's about feelings too

A logical decision may well be a good decision, but it should also take account of your feelings. A decision that is made purely based on logic might lead us to do something that makes sense in principle, but that could make us unhappy in practice. For this reason, it is important that we recognise how we feel about the future.

So, how do you feel about going to university? Consider the following questions.

- What do you feel excited about?
- Which aspects do you feel worried about?
- What do you feel enthusiastic about?
- What do you feel doubtful about?

Now think about any other feelings you may be having.

It is important to be aware of our feelings when we are making important decisions as they can help us to know more about what we really think is important for us and what will make us happy. Remember, if we are happy, we are much more likely to succeed academically and personally.

> Let your dreams influence
> the choice you will make.
> This is the start of the rest
> of your life ...

✏ *Try this*

Now make a list of your feelings about going to university.

Can I do more than I think I can?

It is important to understand that many of us make assumptions that can seriously restrict the way we make decisions. If you have ever found yourself thinking or saying something like 'I could never do that because …', or 'I could never study there because …', you might be right. But, if you examine things a little more deeply, you could find that it is a limiting assumption (Kline, 1999). Many of us are very quick to dismiss ideas, and this can happen for a number of reasons.

Here are some examples.

- It is easier to do this than to take the time to do some careful research.
- We are affected by hearsay – things that people say to us; they seem confident and we believe them, but they will not always be right.
- We lack confidence in our own ability and it's less risky to aim low rather than high.
- Everyone experiences 'knock backs' and some people find it more difficult to recover from these than others.

So, if you have found yourself rejecting things that interest you for reasons like these, it is probably worth revisiting them to see if you have made valid decisions. Remember, sometimes our assumptions are correct but sometimes they aren't. These assumptions can be our way of avoiding challenges that we are capable of overcoming. Facing up to them can be motivating and satisfying.

✏ *Try this*

Now think about a time when you have said or thought 'I couldn't study there because …', or 'I couldn't study that because …'. How do you feel about that now? Was that correct? Or was it a limiting assumption?

THEME 2.5

My next step

Making big decisions is never an easy process. It can feel like 'the stakes are high' and we worry about making mistakes. Applying to university is a lengthy process too, and everything happens when there are lots of other pressures (e.g. deadlines for course work and revision for exams). It is easy to put things off and very tempting to want to think about things later.

With any big decision, it is a good idea to break it down into small parts as this makes it easier to manage. Here are some key steps in the university choice process.

- Research into courses.
- Planning university visits.
- Thinking about finance and other expenses.
- Research into accommodation.
- Considering the pros and cons of taking a gap year.
- Making time to complete a good application.

Taking a step-by-step approach helps a lot as it means you are less likely to feel overloaded.

Think about your future.

🖉 *Try this*

Take a few minutes to consider what you need to think about.
Try ranking the points on the opposite page into an order with
the most important being number one. You may also want to add
your own points to this list too.

✏️ *Further notes*

What should I study?

This section will help you to:

- consider a range of courses on offer
- assess the value of academic and vocational programmes
- think about whether you want to study something new or something familiar
- consider how many subjects you may want to study
- think about the pros and cons of studying full-time or part-time.

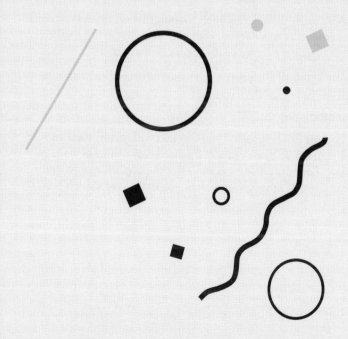

Choosing my course

Deciding what to study is a major part of the university choice process. With so many courses on offer, it can be difficult to fathom out what will suit you best. It is good to start with some key principles and the topics in this section will help you to do this well.

Most universities offer several different kinds of degree, and the main ones are:

- where you focus on one subject (single honours)
- where you study two subjects (joint honours)
- where you study three subjects (triple honours)
- where you study a number of subjects (combined honours)
- where there is a placement year built in (see Theme 9.4)
- where you can spend some time studying abroad
- degree apprenticeships.

In addition, many universities offer courses that are equivalent to the first two years of a degree, with the option of adding a third year later to gain a full degree. Examples of these are:

- Higher National Diploma
- Diploma of Higher Education
- Foundation degree.

These options can be useful if you feel that you do not want to commit yourself to three years of further study from the word go. In addition, Foundation degrees can offer the opportunity to gain work experience, although very often you must have the job first.

🖊 *Try this*

Using a search engine, do some initial internet research to find an example of each of the courses discussed above. Write some notes here on what you find.

Will the course suit me?

An academic or a vocational course?

With so many courses on offer, deciding which course you want to do can be tricky. One key question is whether you would like to do an academic course or a vocational one. Understanding the difference is important and you will also need to consider the pros and cons of each.

- An academic course focuses on a subject or subjects that you study for their own sake. This could be something you currently enjoy or a new subject that you would like to study. This could be a subject that is specialised, and unavailable before university (e.g. anthropology).
  Pros: This gives you the opportunity to study something you love in more depth and at a more challenging level. If you are unsure about what you want to do in the future, this keeps your options open.
  Cons: It will not prepare you for anything specific and you will need to think about getting some experience as well as your degree to add to your CV.

- A vocational course prepares you for an area of work or a career.
  Pros: If you are clear about what you want to do in the future, a course like this could be very helpful. Some jobs are difficult or even impossible to enter without one of these qualifications, e.g. nursing, medicine, dentistry, engineering.
  Cons: It could be difficult if you change your mind and your motivation could drop.

In addition, a vocational course will often be more practical and could include sessions in workshops, studios or laboratories. An academic course could be a mixture of lectures, seminars and tutorials and it is useful to know that the balance can vary from university to university. So, some will ask you to spend more time in lectures while others will focus on seminars and tutorials. When thinking about your course choice, it's good to bear in mind how you learn best.

 *Try this*

Looking at the pros and cons on the opposite page, what kind of course do you feel will suit you best and why?

Something new or something familiar?

It's good to think about whether you want to study something new or continue with something familiar that you enjoy. Again, considering the pros and cons will be important so here are some other questions you may want to think about.

- How will I know if I will enjoy something if I've never studied it before? The short answer to this is, you won't. So, it's important to do some in-depth research to find out more about what it involves. If it is similar to something you have studied before that you enjoy, that will help. It could also involve subjects that you enjoy and are good at (e.g. engineering involves a lot of maths and physics), which is another good sign.

- If it's a subject I've done before, will it involve doing more of the same? To an extent, yes, but you also need to expect to do much more. Also, you could focus on aspects of a subject you have enjoyed, or study the subject more broadly. E.g. a degree course like history can be very broad or can specialise in certain periods of time, like ancient history. Again, some in-depth research will be important to ensure that the course meets your particular interests.

Research is a word that will come up a lot in this book and is a key to making good choices.

 *Try this*

Look at a university prospectus (in a library or online) and list 10 courses that you have not come across before. Now look through the rest of the prospectus. Do any courses appeal to you? If so, what are they?

How many subjects should I study?

Deciding how many subjects to study is a very individual thing. Some people like to delve deep into a subject and want to learn as much as they can about it. Others want more variety and have several strengths that they want to build on. The following questions will help you to identify what is right for you.

- Is there a subject you love that you would like to spend all your time on?
- Which of your subjects might go well together? E.g. two foreign languages, business studies and IT.
- Would you like to add a new subject that is related to one you enjoy? E.g. physics with astrophysics.
- How much variety do you enjoy?

Unless you are one of those people who is really good at lots of different things, it is worth remembering that it can be more difficult to do well across a number of subjects than in one or two. But, if you are someone who has lots of different interests and strengths, then why not go for it? Get the variety that keeps your interest and this will also give you lots of scope for the future.

What should I avoid doing?

 *Try this*

How many subjects would you ideally like to study? Which particular ones appeal to you?

Studying full-time or part-time?

Most people study full-time at university but this is not the only option. You can study in different ways and here are the main ones.

- Full-time – this speaks for itself, but remember that the university academic year is shorter. So even if you are on a full-time course it will probably start in late September or October and finish somewhere around late May to mid-June. However, some professional courses (e.g. nursing) have a longer academic year. Most programmes last three years, but some are longer, e.g. medicine.

- Part-time – this suits some people who cannot study full-time or who want or need to spend longer gaining their degree. For example, some people need to do a substantial amount of paid work to support themselves while they study. Most part-time courses take twice as long to complete as full-time ones (so a three-year full-time course will take six years to complete as a part-time student).

- Blended or distance learning – here most of the work is done online using resources relevant to the subject. People communicate with one another through online discussion boards and students can work much more flexibly. This can be very helpful if you have other commitments such as work and family.

Many universities offer different options for study to make their courses inclusive and accessible to as many people as possible.

 ## *Try this*

Which of the options outlined on the opposite page do you think would suit you best?

✏ *Further notes*

Where should I study?

This section will help you to:

- think about the different types of universities
- find out about how universities are structured and how this can affect their location
- consider how far away from home you would like to be
- consider whether or not you would want to study abroad
- think about how this could affect your academic progress.

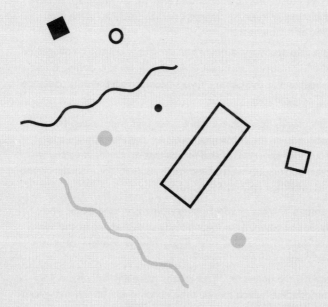

THEME 4.1

What types of university are there?

Universities vary but most fall into one of the following groups.

- Ancient universities – founded before the 1800s (includes Oxford, Cambridge and Edinburgh).
- Red brick – founded in the 19th century in major industrial cities because of the need for more graduates in science and technology. They are often located in city centres and have an undefined campus (includes Manchester, Leeds and Bristol).
- Plate glass or 1960s universities – founded to increase the number of universities; often referred to as campus universities, they were built on green-field sites outside city centres (includes Warwick, Kent and York).
- New universities – originally polytechnics, teacher training or other types of colleges. These were granted university status as part of more recent education reforms, although some have a long history of running degree courses (includes Bath Spa, Cumbria and Chichester).
- You can also study for a degree at university colleges, colleges of higher education and specialist colleges (e.g. for art, drama, music and dance) and at the Open University, which specialises in distance learning programmes.

Universities usually specialise in particular academic areas, so become well known for certain subjects (e.g. Bath for science and Loughborough for sport). This also means that no single university is good at every subject, or even offers every subject. You will also want to consider whether you want to study:

- at a campus university where everything is in one place, and usually out of town. This means living and studying in the same place at least for the first year. Everything is convenient, but it can be intense.
- at a city-centre university. This means travelling daily from your accommodation, which can be time consuming but can give you a greater sense of independence. You also get to know the city better.

Remember, the most important thing in all of this is what will suit you.

🖉 *Try this*

Look at an online prospectus for one university from each of the groups identified on the opposite page. What does this tell you about the kind of university that might be right for you? Which would you prefer – a campus or city centre university – and why?

Will the value of my degree be really affected by the university I choose?

How are universities structured?

Most universities are made up of a number of different faculties that focus on particular subjects. These faculties are divided into schools or departments, and some also have specialised centres. Most faculties are based on one particular campus, although not always. A small number of universities have a college structure (e.g. Oxford, Cambridge and Durham). So, why does any of this matter?

One vital piece of information to find out is where the course you are interested in is being delivered, particularly if the university concerned has more than one campus. So, let's imagine you are interested in studying veterinary medicine. You like the look of Nottingham University because it has an attractive campus on the edge of the city. First it is important to find out which faculty offers the course and this quickly becomes clear when you look at the prospectus. As well as the main campus, the university also has one in Sutton Bonnington in Leicestershire, and this is where the course is delivered. So, rather than studying on the large campus in Nottingham, you will actually be studying on a small campus in the Leicestershire countryside. Finding this out before you apply is obviously vital!

 **Try this**

If you now have some universities in mind, check out their locations and where courses are offered. If you are still unsure, look at the online prospectus for a multi-site university (e.g. Anglia Ruskin, University of Greenwich) and see where the different faculties are located. Make some notes here.

Location, location, location

Where you want to study geographically is an important thing to think about, in particular how far away from home you would like to be. Some people see it as an opportunity to live away from home, to be independent and to experience life in a different part of the country. Others want to have the opportunity to go home at the weekend if they want to, and some prefer to commute each day. There are no right and wrong answers to this and what suits one person will not suit everyone. The most important question here is, what do you want? Here are some pros and cons to think about.

- **Studying a long way from home**
  Pros: more independence; experiencing a completely different place; meeting people from a different part of the country.
  Cons: home-sickness; long journeys from home and back again during breaks, which can also be expensive; very difficult to pop home if you need or want to; losing touch with your friends from home who may not want to travel a long way to visit you.

- **Studying near enough to be able to go home at the weekend**
  Pros: being able to go home whenever you like, but still far enough away to have some independence; keeping in touch with friends who may also be studying near to home; the best of both worlds.
  Cons: people at home may expect you to go back more than you want to; you may miss out on university activities at the weekends; the worst of both worlds.

- **Studying close to home**
  Pros: usually much cheaper than living away; means you can stay in touch with people who are also studying near home; everything is much more familiar.
  Cons: could involve a long commute; missing out on social aspects; less independence.

So, what is important for you?

✏ *Try this*

Type your postcode into a map on the internet. Now add the postcode of a university you may want to apply to. How far away from home is it? Does that sound too near, too far or just about right? What are the transport links like? Now try this with some other universities you are considering.

Would it mean I'd need to move out of home?

Study abroad

As UK tuition fees rise, increasing numbers of students are considering the possibility of studying abroad. Here are some things to bear in mind.

- Studying abroad can offer you an opportunity to experience living in another country and meeting lots of new people.
- It can help you become much more independent.
- It can look great on your CV.
- Unless you are fluent, or are aiming to be fluent, in a particular foreign language, the course will need to be taught in English. However, increasing numbers of degree courses are being taught in English in a range of European countries.
- In certain countries, tuition fees can be lower, but remember all the other costs involved too (see Theme 7.1).
- You may not have access to a student loan if you choose to study abroad.

At the time of writing it is unclear how the UK's decision to leave the European Union will affect your ability to study abroad in Europe. Remember too that you don't have to study abroad for your first degree; there are also postgraduate options abroad for later on if you feel this would suit you better.

✐ *Try this*

The top five choices for study abroad are Australia, Canada, France, Germany and the USA. Look at the Prospects website (www.prospects.ac.uk) for some details and write some notes here. Is studying abroad something you want to consider?

What will make me happy?

This question may sound a bit trite, but if you are happy on your course you are much more likely to succeed than if you are miserable. So, we all need to think about what makes us happy, and in relation to studying it is worth taking a bit of time to think through some key aspects, such as:

- being able to continue doing things I enjoy in my spare time
- the social life I might have
- making new friends easily
- being in a location where I feel comfortable
- being able to get around easily
- the facilities on offer, both in the university and outside.

Some of these will be more important for you than others and you may be able to add some of your own too.

 *Try this*

Write some notes under each of the headings on the previous page.
You can add some headings of your own too.

 *Further notes*

THEME 5

It's time to be strategic

This section will help you to:

- understand what it means to be strategic in the university choice process and why this is important
- understand what university rankings mean
- plan how you will respond to offers of places
- think about how you perform best in assessment processes
- add more detail to your timeline.

What does it mean to be strategic and why is this important?

Being strategic means knowing where you want to get to and planning how you will get there. It means putting yourself in the best possible position to achieve what you want to achieve, and is a vital part of the university choice process.

Here are some steps to help you be strategic.

- Be clear about where you want to get to – hopefully this journal is helping you to get some clarity about what you want and where you would like to study. It's a complex but exciting process.

- Think about the research you would like to do – this makes the process easier. Remember that it helps to talk to others (friends, teachers, parents and carers, and careers advisers) as they will support you.

- Plan the steps you need to take to get there – a step-by-step approach always helps when it comes to big tasks. Breaking it down makes it feel much more manageable.

Completing this section and all the sections in this book will help you to take a strategic approach. So, stick with it and you will definitely see the benefits!

✏️ *Try this*

How are your ideas developing regarding where and what you would like to study? Make some notes here.

What are university rankings?

Every year universities are asked to collect lots of data that is submitted to relevant government agencies for analysis. From this data all universities are ranked according to the scores they receive in the following areas.

- Entry standards – what qualifications do the students have when they start their course?
- Student satisfaction – how satisfied are the students with their course and the university?
- Research quality – how good is the research being undertaken at the university?
- Teaching quality – how good is the teaching?
- Graduate prospects – what do students do after they graduate?
- An overall score – this gives the university its ranking out of 127 universities in all.

University rankings are important and it is understandable that all students would like to go to those that are ranked high on the list. But here are some other things to consider too.

- Not everyone can go to one of the top 10 on the list. These will be the most competitive places to get into, so having a Plan B will be very important just in case.
- People who are applying to Oxbridge (Oxford or Cambridge) can apply to only one or the other in the same admissions round. This is because of the time it takes to interview all applicants.
- Universities that score highly on research often invest more time in this than they do in teaching. This means that you need to be prepared for lots of independent study.
- Those universities lower down the list can be very good in particular subject areas. So, check the rankings by course as well as by institution.

 *Try this*

Using the internet, find a website that shows the latest university rankings. Search for the universities you are interested in and look at their results. Look at the detail in relation to the course you are interested in, too.

What kind of offers will I get?

Getting an offer of a place is always exciting, and university rankings will tell you the grades or the number of UCAS Tariff points people gained who secured a place. Brian Heap's book *University Degree Course Offers* (also available online) is very useful too when looking for this kind of information. Being clear about the kind of offers you might receive will be very important when selecting the universities to include in your application. Here are some tips – and remember, it will often be good to speak to relevant people who will be happy to support and advise you.

- As well as being clear about where you would like to study, you also need to manage the risk – not too much and not too little. This means weighing up your chances of success and making your decisions accordingly.

- Most offers come with conditions – qualifications or numbers of points that you have to get in order to gain entry. How likely are you to get what they might well ask for? There is no point in applying for courses that will ask you for grades that you will not achieve. This could mean that you will get rejections – never a good experience!

- Be careful of playing it safe – everyone wants a place, but if you aim too low you may find yourself on a course that doesn't challenge you enough. So, aim high and in relation to your capabilities, but not too high.

As your offers of places come in, you will need to think about what to do next. By the relevant deadline date you will need to accept one as your firm offer and one as your insurance offer. Being strategic about this will help you to secure your well-earned place. There is no point in accepting a place as your insurance if it is asking for higher grades or more UCAS Tariff points than your firm offer. Your insurance should always be a university asking for lower grades or fewer points, so that you have something to fall back on if you need it.

✏️ *Try this*

Make a list of the courses you are interested in and the grades or number of points they are asking for.

What about assessment?

Finding out how you will be assessed on your course can be an important aspect of choosing your future course. Again, it is important to know yourself well and to be clear about what helps you to succeed. When finding out how you will be assessed, you may want to consider the balance between course work and exams, because:

- some programmes assess only through course work
- others use only exams
- some degrees include practical exams such as design or construction projects, laboratory experiments, computer-aided assessments and multiple-choice papers
- others include presentations and interpersonal assessments such as group work and orals
- some degrees include a dissertation or independent study as part of the final year. This gives students the opportunity to research something they are interested in and can be a good preparation for further study.

If you are doubtful about any of these, do speak to your teachers or tutors to find out where they feel your strengths lie.

✏️ *Try this*

Which type of assessment suits you best? Do you prefer exams or course work? How will you be assessed on your preferred course(s)?

THEME 5.5

Going back to my timeline

In Theme 1.5 you set some goals and devised a timeline. Now is a good time to revisit this in order to add some more details to it. Don't be afraid to make changes to it, as working through this journal may well mean that you are beginning to see things a bit differently.

Having a timeline is helpful as it is a visual reminder of things you need to do. Remember that you can also cross things off – these might be things you have now done or things that you feel you no longer need or want to do.

 *Try this*

How do you feel now when you look at your original timeline? What do you want to add to it? You may even want to devise a new timeline – and don't forget to include a good amount of time in your plans for writing your personal statement.

✏️ *Further notes*

THEME 6

University visits

This section will help you to:

- think about why it is good to visit universities
- consider which universities you want to visit
- make a plan for when you will make the visits
- prepare for university visits
- think about devising some questions to ask while on your visits.

So why visit universities?

So, why is it a good idea to visit universities? Bearing in mind that you are planning to spend at least two, probably three years at university, it is important to know as far as you can that you will be happy there. Of course, you will look at prospectuses when you are doing your initial research, but remember that you need to use these wisely – all the photographs will have been taken on sunny days, with all the best possible views. This is because prospectuses are all about marketing and every university is trying to persuade you to study there.

Here are some reasons why taking some time to visit universities is important.

- It gives you a first-hand view – you will be able to see things for yourself rather than relying on the views of others.
- You will be able to talk to relevant staff – this includes academic staff who will be teaching you and other professional staff too (e.g. accommodation, finance).
- You may be able to talk to students who are studying there already – you will be able to get their honest impressions of what it's like.
- You will be able to see the facilities for yourself – this includes accommodation, the library and sports facilities.
- You will be able to get a feel for whether or not you will be happy there – this sounds very abstract, but there really is no substitute for going and getting a feel for if it's the right place for you or not.
- You will be able to see exactly where it is and how easy or difficult it is to get there from home.

Visiting universities is important, so be sure to make the most of it.

 **Try this**

What do you feel you want to find out when you go on university visits? Make some notes here.

Go to open days to find out more about each uni.

Which universities do I want to visit?

Thinking about which universities you want to visit is important because you probably can visit only a small number. So, you need to be clear about where you want to visit and to make some plans accordingly. Here are some useful tips.

- Be sure to visit those that you have a serious interest in – there is no point visiting somewhere if you feel you are unlikely to go there.

- Don't feel that you have to visit only places close to home – a visit can be a great way of finding out what it might be like to be away from home. It will also help you to see how far away a particular university is and how long it takes to get there.

- You do not need to restrict yourself to open days – universities run other events too, such as tours, applicant days and guided campus visits.

If you are not able to visit, it's worth looking out for any higher education fairs near you. These are events where representatives from a number of universities have stands and are ready to talk to people who want more information. In addition, some universities have online tours which can give you an idea of what it would be like to study there.

 *Try this*

Make a list of the universities you would like to visit and rank them in order of importance.

How to make a plan for university visits

Planning well ahead will be very important if you want to visit a number of universities. Many have a small number of open days per year and you need to book early to be sure of getting a place. If all the places are taken, you will usually need to wait for the next one. Some open days take place at weekends, and if you are travelling some distance you may be able to visit more than one institution over a couple of days. The following points will help you to start planning.

- The first step is to search online for the dates of open days. Several websites show the dates of all open days; this is useful as it saves you a lot of time going through individual university websites. Dates are usually published quite far ahead, so start your planning early.

- Think about who you will go with. You may want to go with family or friends or alone. Going with people can help if you would like to get their impressions too – but remember, in the end it's your thoughts that count because you will go there.

- Be sure to allow enough time to go on a campus tour and to visit different parts of the university concerned.

- If you are going by public transport, book your tickets in advance because this will save you money.

- Don't forget to book a place. Numbers will be limited, so try to book as early as you can.

Visiting universities will be an important part of your decision-making process. Many students say that it's the most important thing they did in the whole process, and in most cases it was very enjoyable too.

 ***Try this***

Now go back to the list of universities you would like to visit and look up the dates of open days and campus tours. Add them to your list to start your planning.

It's all about preparation

Open days are often short and you will usually have to spend some time waiting to see particular people, or for a tour of certain facilities. Here are some points that will help you plan for the day.

- Universities publish timetables for their open days well in advance of the days themselves and it is well worth looking at these in detail to make sure that you see everything you want to see.

- Most open days include a tour of the campus and it is well worth making sure that you have time to do this. Often they happen early in the day, so be sure not to miss out. Also, take some time to wander around by yourself to soak up the atmosphere.

- Most universities offer presentations at particular points in the day, and putting these into your schedule will be important too. These could be presentations about the university as a whole, the course or courses you are interested in, or something more general such as finance and bursaries. Course presentations will also be an opportunity to meet some of the staff who will be teaching you.

Bearing all of this in mind, you will want to make a plan for each visit.

 ***Try this***

Four visit templates are included in Part 3 for you to complete and take with you on your visits. Have a look at them now and make a list of the most important things you want to see and do when on a university visit.

THEME 6.5

What questions do I want to ask?

One of the best parts of a visit is having the opportunity to ask questions directly of the people concerned. This is a big part of getting information first hand. There is nothing worse than finding yourself on your way home and remembering what you meant to ask. For this reason, it is good to think about the questions you want to ask. These questions might be about:

- the course or courses you are interested in, including content, how the course is delivered and the work assessed
- facilities
- accommodation
- finance and bursaries
- employability and what people do following graduation
- placements or opportunities to study abroad.

It is very easy to forget the questions that you want to ask when the time comes, so don't be afraid to write them down. This will show people that you are well prepared and are taking the process seriously.

When visiting universities ask current students' opinions of the place to get a good idea of uni life there.

 ***Try this***

Now devise three key questions you want to ask on university visits.

 *Further notes*

THEME 7

Money and finances

This section will help you to:

- assess the various costs involved in going to university
- consider where it is more expensive or cheaper to study
- understand what a bursary is
- consider what the impact of doing some paid work while studying might be
- understand what a student loan is.

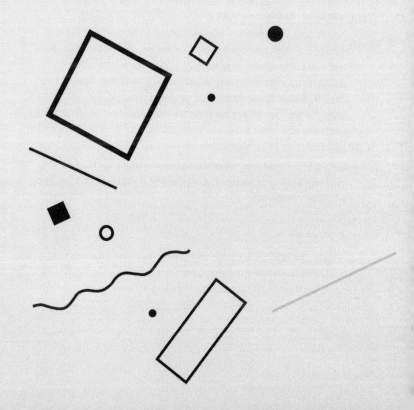

What does it cost to study at university?

There is no doubt that going to university is expensive, and it is good to understand the main financial elements to help your planning. These are as follows.

- Tuition fees – these costs are lower for some courses than others (e.g. Foundation degrees).

- Accommodation – this varies a lot depending on where you study (see Theme 7.2) and whether food is included.

- Food – if you are in self-catering accommodation you will need to factor in the cost of food. On top of that you will need money for lunches and snacks.

- Travel – this needs to include travel to and from home to university, and to and from the campus daily if you are not living nearby. You may want to go home during term time too.

- Books and stationery – you will want to budget for a small number of key textbooks and for things like notepaper, files and pens. Many universities buy access to e-books for their students as well as having multiple copies of key texts in the library. Some bookshops and students' unions also sell second-hand books. So, overall it pays to wait and see which books you use a lot and how available they are before making expensive purchases.

- Insurance – you may need to set aside an amount of money for insuring your possessions, particularly if you will not be living in a hall of residence.

- Social life – a good social life will be important but can be expensive!

All of this can add up to a lot of money, but don't forget that most graduates earn more than most non-graduates, so it's good to think of it as an investment in your future.

✏ *Try this*

Using the headings from the bullet points on the opposite page, start to devise an approximate budget for your studies. Remember, you can get some of the detail you need from university online prospectuses.

Uni or not? You're the one who has to live with the decision.

Is it more expensive to study in some places than others?

Without a doubt the answer to this is yes. Just like life generally, it is cheaper to live in some parts of the country than others. A recent survey showed that, overall, Portsmouth, Liverpool and Newcastle were the cheapest places to study in the UK, and Edinburgh was the most expensive. Students in Oxford and Cambridge pay the most for rent and those in Teesside and Swansea Metropolitan pay the least.

Because accommodation is expensive, some students choose to study close to home to save money. If this is something you are considering, you need to include the cost of daily travel in your calculations. Depending on the distance between where you live and study, this could be considerable, and you also need to think about the time it will take.

Many students do some paid work while they are studying (see Theme 7.4), and this not only helps with their finances but also gives them some valuable things to add to their CV for when they graduate. In the survey above, one of the reasons why Edinburgh came out as the most expensive place to study was because of a lack of available part-time work.

Weighing up the costs of going to university is only one part of making a strategic decision. Going somewhere just because it's cheaper might not be the best decision as it might not offer the course you want or be in the part of the country you would prefer. However, it would be a mistake to ignore the financial side totally.

 **Try this**

Look at the latest surveys on where it is cheapest and most expensive to study. How might this affect your decisions?

What is a bursary?

A bursary is a sum of money available to help with the cost of studying at university. Sometimes these are called scholarships. They are offered to students who fulfil certain criteria, such as:

- if your family income is classified as being low
- if you live in a geographical area where fewer people go to university
- if you are disabled
- if you are excellent at sport
- if you have been in the care of a local authority
- if you are studying for a course in a shortage area
- if you excel in a subject or subjects.

When doing your research, it is well worth looking at the criteria for bursaries as this could be an important factor in your decision making. In addition, a degree apprenticeship can be a good way of avoiding some or all of the debt involved in going to university.

 **Try this**

Now look at the criteria for bursaries for three of the universities you might be interested in applying to, which you will find on their websites. What does this mean for your planning?

THEME 7.4

Should I work while I study?

Many students do some paid work while they study, to help them with the overall costs of going to university. Some choose to work during term time and others find paid work in the holidays. It's worth remembering that university holidays are much longer than school holidays, so there will be a substantial amount of time (particularly during the summer) when you will be able to work either in this country or abroad.

Many students work during term time for their own universities (e.g. in the coffee shops and bars). This makes a lot of sense as these places are busy at this time and students are available for work. Some universities have job agencies (e.g. Unitemps) on campus and these are excellent places to look for job vacancies.

It's good to think about the pros and cons of working while studying.

Pros – it helps with all the costs and gives you more money in your pocket; it adds to your CV; it gives you useful work experience.

Cons – it takes up some of your valuable study time; if your lectures and seminars are spread out across the week, fitting paid work in as well can be difficult; unless you work for your university, an employer may want you to work in the holidays too; it could also affect your social life.

Deciding whether or not to work is an individual thing, and thinking about it beforehand can help you to make this decision further down the line.

> Look at all options – uni, gap year, work.

✐ *Try this*

Think about the pros and cons listed on the opposite page and make some notes under each of them here.

What is a student loan?

A student loan is an amount of money given to you each year to help with the costs of going to university. The money is administered by the Student Loans Company, an organisation that is owned by the government to provide loans and grants to students in the UK. Most students who live in the UK apply to the company for a loan.

Applying for a loan is part of the process of preparing to go to university and it is vital to make sure that you apply for your loan in good time. Missing the deadline would mean a delay in receiving it, which could make the early weeks of being at university difficult. The Student Loans Company pays your tuition fees directly to the university and as part of their loan some students also receive a maintenance loan to help with things like rent and food.

It's good to know that you start paying back your student loan only when you are earning more than a certain amount. The money is then taken straight from your salary – the more you earn, the more you pay off – so in a way it's more like paying tax than paying off a loan. Repayments can be made over a long period, and if you are not earning a lot of money, you won't be paying a lot back. As your salary increases you will pay more, until the loan is paid off.

✎ *Try this*

Now look at the Student Loans Company website and check the deadline date for applying for a loan. Be sure to put this in bold in your timeline to make it stand out. Also, check the current salary threshold for starting to pay the loan back once you graduate.

 *Further notes*

THEME 8

Do I take a gap year?

This section will help you to:

- consider what you might gain from taking a gap year
- think about the pros and cons of taking a gap year
- consider what makes a good gap year
- look at resources for planning a gap year
- think about whether to apply to university this year or next year.

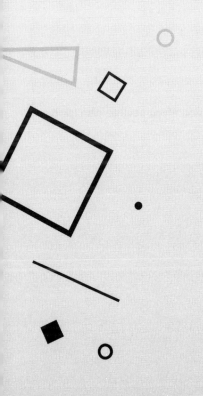

THEME 8.1

What would I gain from taking a gap year?

When thinking about whether to take a gap year, it's good to be clear about what you want to gain from it. People take gap years for different reasons; some people want a break from studying, others want to travel and some want to work to build up their finances.

So, what can you gain from taking a gap year? Here are some ideas, and you may be able to think of more.

- It gives you a different kind of life experience.
- It increases your confidence.
- It makes you more independent.
- It makes starting university easier, as you will be used to meeting new people and going to new places.
- It raises your cultural awareness.
- It improves your skills (e.g. languages, budgeting, planning).
- It gives you work experience.
- It builds your CV for the future.

Taking a gap year is an individual decision – you need to plan for it carefully so that you can make the most of it!

> If I said I wasn't thinking about how much fun I'm going to have, I would be lying!

 **Try this**

If you took a gap year, what would you gain from it?

What are the downsides?

When deciding whether to take a gap year or not, it is good to think about the disadvantages too. Here are some of them.

- It can be difficult to get back into studying after a long break.
- If most of your friends are going straight to university you will be a year behind them.
- Your course or your student finance package may change in the meantime.
- It can be expensive if you plan to travel.
- You may need to defer your place, which is not automatic.
- You need to be well organised or you could end up doing very little, which would not be good for your CV.

Taking some time to think about whether to take a gap year is always a good idea – and don't forget to talk to people as well (e.g. people you know who have done this).

🖋 *Try this*

What are the disadvantages for you in taking a gap year? How does this help you in your decision-making process?

THEME 8.3

What makes a good gap year?

A good gap year is one where you spend time developing yourself and your skills. A good gap year is all of the following.

- Productive – think about what you want to achieve and set yourself some goals.
- Enjoyable – think about the things you love doing.
- Fulfilling – this can include doing things that you are passionate about (e.g. volunteering).
- Challenging – going outside your 'comfort zone' means your confidence can grow.
- Planned – this means you will make the most of it.

Looking forward, using a gap year well can give you lots to add to your CV. Remember that in the future an employer will want to see that you have spent the time productively. Doing paid work to help with finances is also justifiable, and many people need to spend part of the year working and saving in order to travel later.

 *Try this*

What would make a good gap year for you? Use the points on the opposite page to help you.

Planning a gap year

A gap year takes careful planning and needs to be done ahead of time. Here are some questions to think about that will help you to plan your year if you want to travel.

- What do you want to do while you are away?
- When do you want to leave?
- How long do you want to be away for?
- When will you get back?
- Who will you go with?
- How much money will you need?
- How will you finance it?

There are many websites that will help you with your plans, but make sure that they are reputable and take an ethical approach. Fixing the dates is particularly important – and remember that it is good to have some time at home before you go to university for packing and general preparation.

If you want to work, it will be important to update your CV and to apply for jobs before the summer. Remember that job agencies can help you and that many people find jobs through networking with people they know.

 *Try this*

Now look online for websites that can help you to plan for a gap year. Make some notes on the most useful ones.

THEME 8.5

If I want to take a gap year, do I apply to university this year or next year?

This is a question that many students ask, and the answer is, it depends!

If you are applying to university this year with the intention of taking a gap year, it is usually best to be open about this in your application. Universities understand that many students want to have a year out, and see the benefits of it. They are often happy to offer a place for the following year.

But there are some things to check so as to make sure that it is a good decision and that you won't miss out on what you want to do.

- Will the course you want definitely be on offer the following year?
- Are there any plans to change the course?
- Are any changes expected in the coming year regarding funding?

University staff will be happy to answer questions like this at an open day or if you email them.

If you decide to apply the following year, this can give you some more thinking time. Here are some other things to think about.

- Will you have to attend for an interview, and when might this be?
- If you are travelling to remote parts without internet access, who will check your UCAS online profile?

It is particularly important to make sure that you are available to attend an interview. In these circumstances, it can be easier to apply the year before and defer your place to be on the safe side. If you aren't sure about what you want to do, a gap year can give you more time to reach a decision.

 # *Try this*

Write some notes here about the pros and cons of whether to apply to university this year or next year.

It's not that big a deal, you can always wait a year.

 *Further notes*

What about the labour market?

This section will help you to:

- consider what your degree will do for you in the labour market
- identify job roles and sectors where a degree is essential, and some where it isn't
- identify industries and sectors where not having a degree is a barrier to promotion
- think about the value of a course with a placement year
- consider where there are shortages in the labour market.

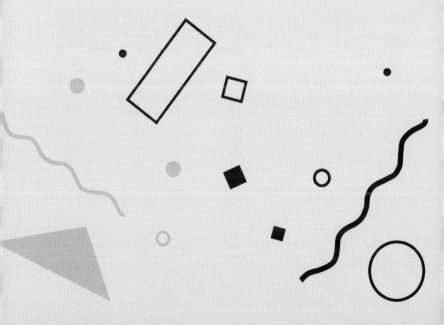

What will my degree do for me in the labour market?

Going to university is a big decision and it is worth understanding something about what your degree can do for you in the future. The government collects statistics each year on what graduates do and how they get on in the labour market. Here are some general statistics that show some consistent overall patterns for graduates.

- They have higher employment rates than non-graduates – they find it easier to find jobs.

- They are more likely to find highly skilled work – the work they do is usually more interesting and challenging.

- They are less likely to be unemployed – they are more likely to keep their jobs, and in times of recession they find other work more quickly.

- They earn more than non-graduates – both average starting salaries and earnings over a lifetime are higher than for those without degrees.

Obviously, there are no guarantees that a degree will do all of this for you as an individual, but statistics show that the likelihood is that it will. So, particularly in relation to money, it is good to think about your degree as an investment in your future. Don't forget all the other things that your experience of going to university will do for you too, such as building your confidence and helping you to grow in independence – some of this can be priceless!

 *Try this*

Visit the Higher Education Statistics Agency's (HESA) website (www.hesa.ac.uk) and look at the latest statistics on graduate employment. If you find these in a long report, just read the Executive Summary at the beginning to get an overall impression.

Will I definitely need to have a degree for certain jobs or industries?

In some job areas having a degree is essential, and without one it will simply be impossible to gain entry. Many jobs at a professional level demand a degree, such as:

- jobs where you study for a degree in that area, e.g. medicine, dentistry, architecture, physiotherapy, pharmacy
- jobs where you need to do some postgraduate or professional study after gaining a degree to gain entry, e.g. law
- jobs where you either need a degree in the subject, or some subject-specific postgraduate study following a degree, e.g. teaching, social work.

However, some industries do not always ask for a degree, e.g. retail, advertising, media. Some of these employers offer good opportunities for people without degrees and you can still make progress to more senior levels, with experience. One important thing to remember though, is that when applying for jobs like this, you will no doubt find yourself in competition with graduates. However, it will probably be cheaper for them to employ you as a non-graduate, which can be an advantage.

✏️ *Try this*

If you have a career interest, do some research on the entry requirements and make some notes here. If you are unsure about what you want to do in the future, look at the Prospects website under 'What can I do with my degree?' Click on the subject you might be interested in studying and look at the career suggestions. Again, make some notes here.

Could not having a degree be a barrier to my career progression?

There are many examples of industries and sectors where not having a degree will be a barrier to your progression. Without a degree, you could find yourself stuck at a certain level and unable to move up any further. This is often referred to as technician level. Here are some examples from a range of industries.

- Engineering – entering employment after A levels or equivalent means that you will be trained at technician level, which often means assisting engineers on projects and doing more practical activities such as maintenance. You cannot be a professional chartered engineer without a degree in engineering.

- Law – after A levels or equivalent, you can be employed as a legal executive, supporting a solicitor, but you will need a degree and a postgraduate qualification to become a solicitor.

- Accountancy – you can become an accounting technician after A levels or equivalent, but will need to study at degree level to become a professionally qualified accountant.

However, while you might only get so far without a degree, some employers will sponsor excellent people to study for a degree or higher level qualification to help them progress. This is particularly the case in shortage areas, such as engineering and technology.

✏️ *Try this*

Now do some internet research into the qualifications needed for these industries: media, advertising, forensic science, civil engineering and physiotherapy. Which of these demand a degree, and are there some that don't?

Should I do a degree with a placement year?

It is well known that a degree on its own no longer guarantees anyone a job; graduates need work experience too. So, a degree course with a placement year can be a very good option and can offer a good opportunity to continue to build your CV and prepare you for the future. Some writers suggest that students who undertake placements gain better degree classifications and others say that high-achieving students are the ones who tend to get good placements (Driffield et al., 2011).

Many universities offer a wide range of courses with the option of doing a placement. If you like the idea of this, here are some things to consider.

- Some universities offer more support than others with finding a placement.
- Universities often charge a fee for the placement year, which adds to the cost of the degree.
- Good placements can be difficult to find and this will take time away from your studies.
- You will graduate a year later than some others who started at the same time as you.

In spite of all of this, a placement year can be a very good option for a range of reasons, in particular helping you to prepare for what you will do after you graduate.

✏️ *Try this*

How do you feel about a course with a placement year? What would be the pros and cons for you?

Where are the shortages in the labour market?

The labour market in the UK has experienced shortages of staff in certain areas at particular times. It would be a mistake to say that there are always shortages in some areas, but statistics show that some sectors have experienced shortages over a consistent period of time. Here are the main ones.

- Engineering – most types of engineering have experienced shortages over a number of years. This is particularly because of the falling numbers of students studying physics and other sciences at A level or equivalent. Shortages here have been described by some as chronic.

- Information technology – progress in this area of employment is very fast, with new applications being developed all the time. Well-qualified staff are in very high demand.

- Nurses – particularly well-qualified specialist nurses (e.g. those who work in operating theatres and intensive care) are in very short supply.

Other shortages in the labour market can be temporary. Sometimes this is based on how well the economy is doing at the time, or a range of other factors. For example, the building industry is usually the first to suffer when the economy goes into recession, but the first to pick up when things get better; or there can be shortages in teaching a few years after an increase in the birth rate.

Overall, it is useful to bear in mind where the shortages might be in the labour market. But basing your decisions only on this may not be a good idea.

✏ *Try this*

Use a search engine to find current reliable newspaper articles on labour market shortages. How might this affect your decisions?

 *Further notes*

THEME 10

What if things don't go according to plan?

This section will help you to:

- understand what happens if you don't get the grades you need
- consider the options open to you
- be ready for the Clearing process
- understand what a Foundation year is and why this might be a useful option
- think about what to do if your grades are higher than expected.

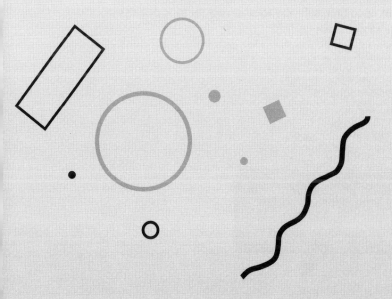

What happens if I don't get the grades I need?

Having gone through the process of applying to university, hopefully you will have received some offers and decided which to accept firmly and which as an insurance. Then it is a case of waiting for your results. So, looking ahead, what if things do not go your way and you don't get the grades or points you need?

First – try not to panic. Receiving news like this is always upsetting, but you need to keep a level head and act quickly.

Second – check UCAS Track to make sure that you don't have an offer. In some circumstances universities still give places even when students haven't quite got the grades or points asked for. Sometimes they may offer a place on a similar course too.

Third – check your insurance offer. If you have planned this wisely, and they have offered you lower grades or fewer points, you may find that they have offered you a place. Again, check UCAS Track.

Fourth – get some support and advice. Many schools and colleges are open on results day for this very purpose. Go in early and don't be afraid to ask for help.

Don't worry if everything doesn't go your way straight away.

✏️ *Try this*

Make a plan of the steps you will take if things don't turn out as you expect. Who will you go to for support?

What options do I have?

Once you get your results, everything will quickly fall into place if they are the results you need. But if not, there will be very little time to act, so it is good to think ahead just in case. So, what will your options be?

- Apply for places at other universities through Clearing (see Theme 10.3).
- Appeal your grades if you feel that you have a case. You will need to discuss this with staff at your school or college and you will need to inform the university that gave you the offer that you accepted firmly.
- Take a gap year and apply again next year. You will have your results already and can target universities that should offer you a place.
- Retake the year to improve your grades and apply again next year.
- Consider working to gain experience to add to your CV.

It's always difficult when things don't go according to plan. But remember that you do have options and can still be successful via another route.

🖉 *Try this*

Think about the options listed on the opposite page. If you didn't get the grades or points you needed, what would your preferences be? Make a list of the pros and cons.

How can I prepare for the Clearing process?

Once A level results come out, Clearing can be a very fast process, so it is good to be well prepared just in case. Here are some pointers.

- If you can, make sure that you are at home on A level results day. Being away on holiday can put you at a serious disadvantage.

- Make a shortlist of the universities you would like to approach if you have to do so. Start with those that you have applied to already; you have already done some research on these and know that you would be happy to go there. Also, the universities can see that you have thought about going there and that you are not making random decisions.

- Now make a long list in case these don't have any places available.

- Be ready to act quickly. Many free places go on the first day of Clearing.

- At the time, look at the lists of places available on the internet.

- Make sure that your phone is fully charged and get ready to speak to people. Most universities have Clearing helplines that you will need to call. Be clear about the courses you are interested in and the results you have.

- Be ready to go and visit or attend an interview if necessary.

Applying for places through Clearing can be hectic. If you find yourself in this position, it's time to stop procrastinating and hesitating, and to go and get that place!

✎ *Try this*

Make a list of the universities you would like to approach in Clearing if you have to do so.

What is a Foundation year?

Many universities offer a Foundation year for students who have not quite got the grades or points needed for their chosen course. They also offer them to students who do not have the right academic subjects for entry to their chosen degree, or who need support with learning English. So, what is a Foundation year and why might it be a good option?

A Foundation year is a year of study that prepares you for starting a degree course. It will help you to develop your academic and study skills, while exploring your course options. People who study on a Foundation year often have a broad range of backgrounds and experiences and can include people who:

- don't meet the entry requirements for the degree but have the potential to succeed
- don't have the right combination of subjects for direct entry to their chosen degree course
- don't yet know what they want to specialise in
- have had a gap in their education.

Some universities guarantee their Foundation year students an interview for their chosen course at the university. Doing a Foundation year will mean an extra cost, but it could help you to achieve your goals.

🖊 *Try this*

Do some internet research to check out the cost of a Foundation year at the universities where you have accepted offers. How would you feel about this as an option if you needed it?

What if my grades are higher than I expected?

Of course, some people get very good news on results day and do better than they expected. So, what do you do if this happens? You can celebrate the fact that you will soon be off to university. But if you want to, you can now apply for places at other universities through the UCAS Adjustment process. You will be eligible for this if your firm offer of a place has been confirmed and you have exceeded the conditions of it. Here are some important points.

- The Adjustment process is open for only five days following the release of results, so, like Clearing, you must act quickly.

- Just because you can apply to other universities does not mean that you should.

- Unlike Clearing, there is no list of vacant places. You will need to check university websites and ring the universities directly.

- Try not to make a snap decision. Many universities have open days the weekend after results are released, so do go along.

- Don't turn down your original place until you know that you have another one.

- Make sure that you discuss things with someone, e.g. a careers adviser or teacher.

Whether you are going through Clearing or Adjustment, be sure to check things like accommodation and student finance to make sure that you have everything in place.

✏️ *Try this*

What would you do if your results were better than you expected?
Write some notes here.

> What if I choose
> the wrong uni?

✏️ *Further notes*

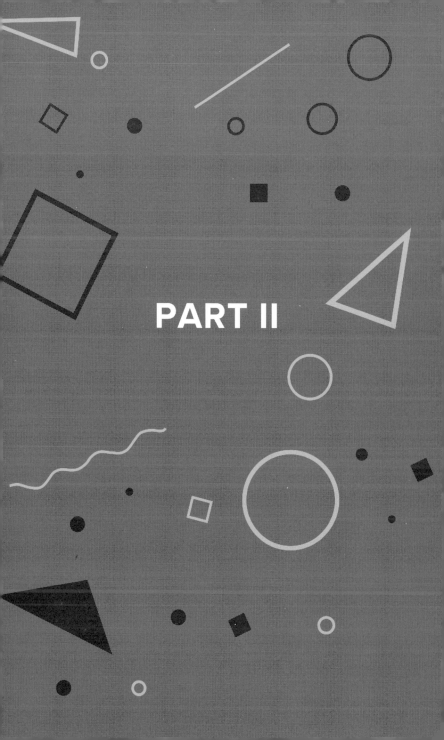

PART II

More space for reflection

Part II gives you some more space for reflective writing and contains a number of activities for you to complete in order to develop your thinking further. Some of these pose questions to help you to think about the big picture, others ask you to imagine a time in the future to help you to think about where you might be heading. This is all designed to help you to think in more depth as you figure out what's next.

✏️ *Try this*

What do you feel about the prospect of going to university? Make a list of positives and negatives.

How big a change is it?

 *Try this*

What is 'a good university'? How would you define this?

✏️ *Try this*

Think about how you learn best. Which would suit you better – a course that has lots of lectures or one that focuses on seminars and tutorials?

✎ *Try this*

What do you hope a degree will do for you in the future?

Don't leave your personal statement to the last minute.

 **Try this**

Imagine it's three or four years from now and you are graduating. What do you see?

I want to feel at home when I'm away.

 *Try this*

Imagine you are on a gap year. Make a month-by-month plan for what you might be doing and where you might be.

 *Try this*

Who can help and support you with your decisions?

How hard is it moving on from A levels?

🖊 *Try this*

Make a note of the contacts that you still have with students who have left and gone on to university. Contact them to see how they are getting on. If you have difficulties knowing who to contact, ask a teacher for some help.

✎ *Try this*

How can you find the information you need? Make a list of reliable and unreliable sources.

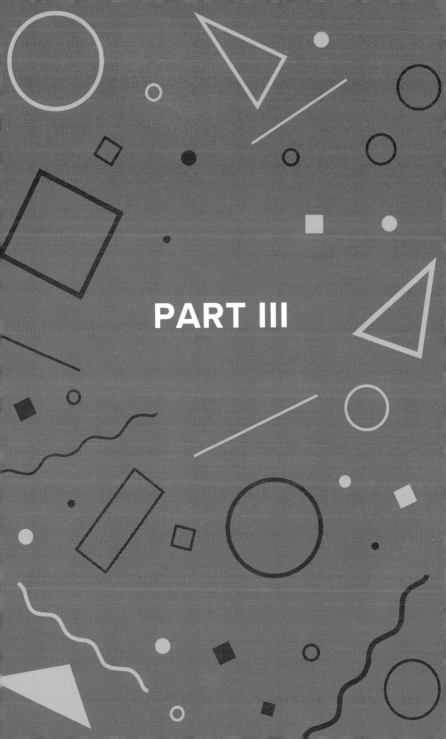

PART III

Notes and records

Part III gives you some space for keeping important notes and records of things. During the university choice process, you will gather lots of information and it will be helpful to keep important things in one place. This part of the Journal can be used for that. It also gives you some space to record notes on key events, such as university visits.

Diary of events

During the coming months, there will be a lot to keep track of.
Insert your key deadlines into the table below and remember to
include things such as university open days and visits, as well as
deadlines for completing your personal statement, applications and
accepting offers.

20◼◻	EVENTS	DEADLINES
September		
October		
November		
December		
January		
February		
March		
April		
May		
June		
July		
August		

20 ⬛⬛	EVENTS	DEADLINES
September		
October		
November		
December		
January		
February		
March		
April		
May		
June		
July		
August		

My personal statement

Ian Stannard's book *How to Write a Winning UCAS Personal Statement* gives lots of helpful advice on writing your personal statement. It can be a difficult and time-consuming thing to write, so be sure to allow yourself plenty of time. Here is some space to write some notes under some headings that will help as you start your preparation.

Opening paragraph

Why this course/subject area?

Academic strengths

Interests

Activities and experience outside education

Key achievements

Closing statement

Pro forma for university visit 1

Name of university	
Date of open day/visit	
Place booked	Yes/No
Travel arrangements	
Course(s) of interest and faculty	
Schedule for the day	
- tour of campus	
- presentation	
- accommodation	
- finance	
- sports facilities	
- other	
Specific questions to ask (aim for at least 3)	
1.	
2.	
3.	
4.	
5.	
6.	
Notes	

Pro forma for university visit 2

Name of university	
Date of open day/visit	
Place booked	Yes/No
Travel arrangements	
Course(s) of interest and faculty	
Schedule for the day	
- tour of campus	
- presentation	
- accommodation	
- finance	
- sports facilities	
- other	
Specific questions to ask (aim for at least 3)	
1.	
2.	
3.	
4.	
5.	
6.	
Notes	

Pro forma for university visit 3

Name of university	
Date of open day/visit	
Place booked	Yes/No
Travel arrangements	
Course(s) of interest and faculty	
Schedule for the day	
- tour of campus	
- presentation	
- accommodation	
- finance	
- sports facilities	
- other	
Specific questions to ask (aim for at least 3)	
1.	
2.	
3.	
4.	
5.	
6.	
Notes	

Pro forma for university visit 4

Name of university	
Date of open day/visit	
Place booked	Yes/No
Travel arrangements	
Course(s) of interest and faculty	
Schedule for the day	
- tour of campus	
- presentation	
- accommodation	
- finance	
- sports facilities	
- other	
Specific questions to ask (aim for at least 3)	
1.	
2.	
3.	
4.	
5.	
6.	
Notes	

Interview preparation

Here are some common interview questions. Make some notes under the headings.

What made you apply for the course?

Which aspects will you find most interesting?

Which aspects will you find the most challenging?

What made you choose this particular university?

What is your greatest achievement to date?

If we asked your friends to describe you, what would they say?

What might you do following your degree?

Offers received

OFFER RECEIVED	GRADES/ POINTS	PROS	CONS	DECISION
University 1				
Yes/No				
University 2				
Yes/No				
University 3				
Yes/No				
University 4				
Yes/No				
University 5				
Yes/No				

Useful websites

Make a list here of any useful websites you find.

REFERENCES

Bassot, B., Barnes, A. and Chant, A. (2014) *A Practical Guide to Career Learning and Development: Innovation in Career Education 11–19*, Abingdon: Routledge.

Covey, S. (2004) *The 7 Habits of Highly Effective People*, London: Pocket Books.

Driffield, N.L., Foster, C.S. and Higson, H.E. (2011) 'Placements and degree performance: do placements lead to better marks, or do better students choose placements?' in D. Siva-Jothy (ed.), *ASET Annual Conference 2011: Research Papers from Placement and Employability Professionals' Conference 2011*, ASET, Sheffield (UK), pp. 4–27, ASET Annual Conference, Leeds, United Kingdom, 6–8 September.

Heap, B. (published annually) *University Degree Course Offers*, Bath: Trotman Education.

Kline, N. (1999) *Time to Think*, London: Ward Lock.

Stannard, I. (2016) *How to Write a Winning UCAS Personal Statement*, Bath: Trotman Education.

INDEX